KidCaps Presents

The Great Depression:
A History Just for Kids

KidCaps is An Imprint of BookCaps™
www.bookcaps.com

© 2012. All Rights Reserved.

Table of Contents

About KidCaps

KidCaps is an imprint of BookCaps™ that is just for kids! Each month BookCaps will be releasing several books in this exciting imprint. Visit are website or like us on Facebook to see more!

Introduction

The temperature is about 40 degrees on this cold November morning. It's only 6:30 AM, but a line has already formed outside of the kitchen. One by one, the men come from different directions and place themselves at the back of the line. They shuffle back and forth, from one foot to the other, trying to keep warm. Their noses can smell the freshly brewed coffee and the hot doughnuts as they are served to the men ahead of them. One by one, the men enter the kitchen, have a quick bite to eat, and then head out to the street. They fan out and go from business to business, looking for work. At the end of the day, they come back here to this line and wait their turn for a small bowl of soup.

All of these men are Americans. Some of them have moved in from the far away farms and small towns that they were born in. Because there is no work back home, they have moved to the city, leaving their families behind, to try and earn some money. Some of them have rented hotel rooms, but others are sleeping on the streets or in little temporary shacks in communities called "Hoover towns". Life is hard for these men, and it doesn't look like things are going to be getting better anytime soon.

It is the United States in the 1930s and these men are experiencing life during what came to be known as the Great Depression. It was a time in the United States when it was hard to find a job. Even people who had jobs made very little money; sometimes, they didn't even make enough to feed their families or themselves. No one was quite sure what exactly the government should do to help, and the two men who served as President during those years had different ways of handling the situation.

Worse yet, the economic problems that began in the United States soon spread to other countries. As we will see, the world was completely changed by the Great Depression of the 1930s. In this report, we will have a close look at what caused the Great Depression, why it lasted so long, and what finally made it end. We will see what it was like to live through it and what some of its lasting effects on people of different countries were. We will try to see the different options that the Presidents had, and even some of the mistakes that they made.

In this report, we will also learn some new vocabulary. First, we will be talking about the **Stock Market**, and why it was and still is so important to the national economy. We will talk about the **gold standard**, and what it meant for governments and their citizens for many years. We will also look at the **New Deal**, which was a series of laws and acts passed by President Franklin Delano Roosevelt to try and end the Great Depression.

Although many of the people who lived during the Great Depression have since died, it was still a very important time in American history. It changed forever the role of the Federal Government in the lives of its citizens, and it helped us to learn a lot about what makes an economy stronger or weaker. Even though 1930 might seem like a long time ago for you, the lessons that were learned back then should be important to you now and in the future.

Are you ready to learn more? Then let's start at the beginning, by learning about the United States Stock Market and the Roaring Twenties.

Chapter 1: What led up to the Great Depression?

After World War I had ended, the American people were very happy that life was getting back to normal and celebrated. Soldiers came home and started to work and to raise their families. Technology was getting better and better each year, and that meant that there were more and more jobs to be had working in large production factories, where radios, cars, and other household items were manufactured. With so many people listening to the same radio stations, advertisements were broadcasted to make people want to buy the same products. As a result, factory production went up, which meant that everyone made more money, which made them buy more, which meant more work, and so on. Economically, things were going very well.

As music became more and more popular (because technology made it easier to record and broadcast music coast to coast) people began, for the first time, to go out and dance in nightclubs. As industry kept growing, the populations in large cities grew, and it was during this period that the majority of Americans became city dwellers, not small town country folk (as they had almost always been before). With so much change in the air and so much money in their pockets, a lot of Americans thought that the good times would never end. This time period was called the Roaring Twenties.

Large companies were quick to take advantage of all of this money floating around. They began to sell shares of companies for higher and higher prices at the United States Stock Market. Do you know what a share is? Do you know what the Stock Market is? Let's find out.

Whenever a business wants to grow, it has to find investors, who are people that are willing to give the business the money that it needs. In return, the investors get a part of the business' profits (if there are any). Somewhere along the way, someone got the bright idea to divide up a company into "shares" or "stocks" (words that refer to a "portion" of a business). Each share would represent a certain percentage of the profits. Men (called "brokers") would gather in downtown New York City and sell these shares to interested investors. If the company did well and made a lot of profits, the shares would become worth lots of money, because they would pay the investors lots of money each year (the portion of interest paid to an investor is called a "dividend"). Eventually, the brokers for these large companies moved their business into a building, and the New York Stock Exchange on Wall Street (in lower Manhattan) was born.

A lot of people began to look at the New York Stock Exchange (often called the "Stock Market") as a way to make some money. However, while some people invested in just one or two companies, others would buy and sell large numbers of stocks each day, depending on the stock's value. Some people even made working on the Stock Market their entire life.

Do you remember what was happening in the national economy during the 1920s? That's right! Things were going really, really well for most Americans. Everybody had jobs, companies were growing, and there was plenty of money to be made. Because companies were making such large profits, the prices of their shares were rising and rising. More investors began to put large amounts of money into the Stock Market. They would buy when the price of a share was low, let it get higher, and then sell the shares for a profit. However, something began to happen in the national economy in the year 1929; it was called a recession. Do you know what a recession is?

National and international economies move like the waves of the ocean: they go up and down. There are a lot of factors that make economies go up and down, including politics, supply and demand, and even the attitude of the people who are working and living in the country. These little up and down movements are perfectly normal. When there is growth in an economy, it is called an "expansion". When that growth stops, and things start to slow down, it is called a "recession". That's what started to happen in the summer of 1929. Companies began to produce less, wages stopped going up, and there weren't as many new jobs. People decided to start saving some of their money instead of spending. None of this was anything to worry about; after all, like we mentioned earlier, recessions are pretty normal. However, the Stock Market began behaving very strangely during the recession of 1929.

Do you remember what makes the price of a company's stock go higher or lower? Well, it depends on how well the company itself is doing and how much money it is making for its investors (who are called "shareholders"). When there is economic expansion, the company makes more money, and the prices of the shares rise, because the investors are getting richer. When there is an economic recession, the company makes less money, the price of the shares go down, because the investors aren't making as much money.

However, in the summer of 1929, when the U.S. economy entered into a recession, the prices of the stocks did not go down as they were expected to do; instead they kept on going higher and higher. This was kind of strange, and a lot of people wondered what was happening. Even though most of the large factories were making fewer products and had less money, the prices of their shares were through the roof. Economists (people who study financial markets and economies) call a situation like this a "bubble". Why? Well, think about it. Have you ever blown a bubble with gum or with some soapy water? What happens when it gets too big?

It bursts.

That's what happened with the Stock Market in 1929. Let's find out more.

Chapter 2: Why did the Great Depression happen?

As we have seen so far, the Great Depression actually started out as a perfectly normal recession during the summer of 1929. However, there were several factors that made this normal recession become something so large and devastating, eventually leading people to call it the "Great Depression". These factors were:

- **The Stock Market crash of October 29, 1929**
- **The use of the gold standard**
- **The dust bowl**
- **The actions of Presidents Herbert Hoover and Franklin Delano Roosevelt before and during the crisis**

The Stock Market crash of October 29, 1929. As we saw earlier, the Stock Market was behaving very strangely during the summer of 1929. Although the prices of shares should have been going down because of the recession, the stock prices just kept going up and up. Why was this? Well, a lot had to do with the fact that investors couldn't believe that the Stock Market would ever stop growing. In fact, many people had begun to "speculate" in the Stock Market. What does the term "speculate" mean? Well, instead or standard long term investing, it has to do with looking for a quick profit from a stock. It is when a person buys a stock one day, hoping to make a profit in a short time, and then turns around and sells it just hours or days later after the price has gone up enough. In the United States, investors began to borrow money from banks in order to speculate on stocks. This created a false value in the Stock Market. Even though the values of company stocks were going higher and higher, there was no real production and no profits to back up that value. It was like a bubble that was getting too big.

Do you remember what happens to a bubble when it gets too big? That's right, it explodes. That's what happened with the Stock Market. When Americans began to take a look around, they realized that there was no reason why stocks should be so high. What's more, there was a new law about to be passed (called the Smoot–Hawley Tariff Act) that would severely limit the production of large factories, which meant that profits would be even lower in the future than they were during the recession. On October 24, 1929, a huge number of stocks were traded or sold on Wall Street, and the country got scared, realizing that the whole system was very fragile. Over the weekend, newspapers all talked about, and on five days later, on Tuesday, October 29, the Stock Market crashed. What was the result? The value of most stocks had gone down by about 89%. What did that mean for the average investor?

For an example, let's say that you were a hardworking factory employee in 1929. Like many workers, you may have made around $1500 per year at your job. But, like many factory employees, you may have jumped onto the bandwagon and borrowed some money to speculate in the stock market. If you decided to borrow $5000 from a bank and then used it to speculate on $5000 worth of stock just before the crash, what would have happened? Well, one week after you bought the stocks, they would only have been worth $550. You would have lost $4450 in one week! That would be the same as about three years' worth of wages at the factory! How would you ever earn that money back? How would you pay off your debt to the bank? Worse yet, as a result of the crash of the stock market, many factories were forced to lay off their employees, which meant that they couldn't pay back the money they owed to the banks. Because of this, some people lost their homes, their cars, everything they owed, and were left with nothing.

The Great Depression had begun.

The use of the gold standard. Another factor that made the Great Depression so strong and so devastating was the gold standard. Do you know what the gold standard was? Well, in order to understand what the gold standard was, we have to understand a little bit about where money comes from.

Money in the Unites States is printed by a central bank called the Federal Reserve. They are in charge of determining how much money is printed and how much the money is worth. After all, if there is too much money floating around, then each dollar will have less buying power. A soda, instead of costing one dollar, might cost five. The Federal Reserve has always tried very hard to make sure that they do their job well.

For many years, the Federal Reserve only printed money based on the amount of gold that was kept in its storehouse. For example, dollars were originally printed with the words: "gold coin" on them. This was to show that each bit of currency in the national economy was backed up by something real and valuable: gold. It also made it clear that U.S. currency could be exchanged at a local bank at any time for real gold coins. Other countries around the world that wanted to do business with the United States had to do the same thing: they had to make sure that their currency was backed up by the gold that they had in their storehouse. If there was no more gold, then no more money could be printed. That way, it would be easy to trade with other countries, because their money would all be similar in value.

However, when people began to get worried about the value of a country's currency, they would go to their local bank and say: "Take your paper money bank, and give me my gold!" Then, they would hide the gold until they thought the economy had gotten through the recession. However, what would have happened if everyone in every country got really scared and didn't trust the government anymore? What would have happened if everyone wanted their gold back at the same time? Well, we found out in 1929. When nations around the world saw that the United States' economy was failing, it began to affect theirs also. After all, much of their business depended on buying and selling with Americans. Citizens everywhere began to demand gold for their currency, which put banks in a bad position.

The gold standard had been a method used by governments to stabilize the value of their currency, but it also meant that governments couldn't print any more money if there was a need unless they found more gold somewhere. When citizens lost confidence in the banks and take all their money away, the government couldn't do anything about it, and would go broke, not even having enough money to keep the basic programs functioning. That is what happened during the Great Depression. The gold standard made it more difficult to get money into the economy and dragged other nations down with the United States.

The dust bowl. Life during the Great Depression was tough enough for people who had been working in factories and who had been living in the big city; they found themselves with no jobs and with no money to pay back their debts. However, people living in the Midwest (mainly farmers) had a difficult time too. Their problems came from a severe drought during the mid-1930s. What made this drought different?

Before settlers moved West during the 1800s, different types of grass and small plants had kept the topsoil from blowing away in the strong winds that roll over the plains in the Midwest (in places like Oklahoma). These plants and grasses had even held onto water in times of drought. However, as farmers began to try to take advantage of every square inch of land that was available to them, they pulled out all of the grass and little plants to make more room for crops. What's more, they never gave the land a rest from one season to the next; they just kept planting and harvesting, planting and harvesting. As a result, when the drought came, the land literally just disappeared: it blew away in the wind. The storms were called dust storms, and they severely damaged the farmland of the Midwest during the 1930s, making life impossible for farmers and agricultural workers. This time period came to be called the "Dust Bowl" and made many farmers leave their farms and move to other states and cities to try and find work.

The actions of Presidents Herbert Hoover and Franklin Delano Roosevelt before and during the crisis. Although each of these men tried their best to make the right decisions during a difficult time, they each ended up making the normal recession of 1929 turn into the ten-year Great Depression.

President Herbert Hoover was the first to contribute to the problem. In May 1929, he had to decide whether or not to sign into law a bill that had just been passed by Congress called the "Smoot–Hawley Tariff Act". What was the purpose of this bill? It would add a tariff (an extra fee) to any products imported from other countries. The goal was to protect American workers from foreign competition by making it more difficult to import and purchase foreign-made goods. The price on some items rose by over 60% (as an example: a car made in Germany that normally sold for $2000 would now sell for $3200, with the government getting the extra money). Why do we say that the Smoot–Hawley Tariff Act contributed to the Great Depression?

When President Hoover signed the bill into law on June 17, 1930, the Great Depression had already begun. However, by signing this bill, Hoover made other trading partners (like Canada, Britain, France, and Germany) very angry. They felt that they were being discriminated against and that no one would buy their products anymore. In a kind of revenge, these other nations all passed legislation putting tariffs on American-made goods. As a result, American factories suffered, because no one in other countries would buy their products. As we see, the Smoot–Hawley Tariff Act ended up being a very bad thing. Yes, by trying to help American workers, it actually ending up hurting them.

President Franklin Delano Roosevelt also committed his share of errors. When a recession (or a depression) hits an economy, the most important thing is to spend money and to get people working. Even though it sounds strange (because most people think that *saving* money is the most important thing during a recession) spending money is what creates jobs, which in turn creates more money, which creates more jobs, etc. So the Federal government should have been spending lots of money in order to help the nation. Although a lot of programs were created to help Americans (as we will see later) not enough money was spent, and America still decided to stick to the gold standard, which made it harder to pay off old debts. Although these situations would later be corrected, President Roosevelt, by not taking the correct actions soon enough, helped to make the Great Depression worse than it had to be.

Now that we understand a little more about what led up to the Great Depression, let's see what actually happened during it.

Chapter 3: What happened during the Great Depression?

During the Great Depression, as we have seen, jobs disappeared and production slowed down. As a result, even the people who were able to keep their jobs were making less money than they had been before. But the individual citizens and large corporations weren't the only ones to suffer: the local and national banks suffered as well. Do you remember that many Americans took out large loans from banks in order to speculate in the Stock Market? Well, when the Stock Market crashed, the stocks went down in value. During the following Depression, people lost their jobs and there was no way that they could ever pay back those large loans. The banks, like any other business, needed money in order to keep operating. They couldn't stand to lose thousands and thousands of dollars and still keep their doors open. One by one, these banks, both large and small, began to go out of business.

This caused a huge panic for the American people. Many Americans still had a little bit of money left over after the Stock Market crash, and they desperately needed that money to survive. However, when they saw that some banks were closing their doors, people all across the country started what's called a "bank run". Do you know what a bank run is? It is when everybody goes to the bank at the same time to take their money out. The problem is this: the bank doesn't actually have enough money to give it to everyone all at once. A lot of the money that had been deposited is loaned out to other businesses or invested in the Stock market. So when all of the people came at once demanding their money, the banks had to find a way to make it happen.

During the Great Depression, bank runs began in October of 1930, one year after the Stock market crash. During the ten year depression, over 11,000 (almost half) of the nation's banks closed their doors for good.

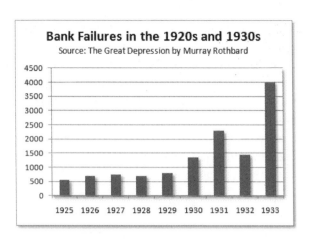

Bank Failures in the 1920s and 1930s

Source: The Great Depression by Murray Rothbard

When there is a bank run, the bank must call in (ask for) all of its loans to be repaid at the same time, even if the person was not expecting to pay it back so soon. Even if some of the larger businesses could have afforded to do this, it would have slowed down their production greatly and made them even less profitable, thus contributing to continuing the depression. It was a lose-lose situation.

During the Great Depression, bank runs became a common item in the newspapers as people everywhere lost their confidence in the economic system. They felt that the safest thing to do was to withdraw all of their money and hide it at home, spending as little as possible. But, what do you think? Is that really the best way to help the economy to recover? No! In fact, those people needed to just leave their money at the banks. That way, the banks could give that money to businesses as loans, which would in turn help those businesses to create more jobs. The Americans living back then needed to do something else: they needed to keep spending their money at local businesses and factories, which would help to increase national production and to put more money into everyone's pockets. Unfortunately, as we have seen, people panicked and that is not what happened.

Because no one really knew how to handle the Great Depression, a lot of Americans suffered. When they lost their jobs, homeowners could no longer afford to pay the loans to the bank for the house that they had bought. As a result, lots of people were evicted from (asked to leave) their own homes. Where could they go with no job and no home? While some people migrated west to places like California to look for work, others just had to make do with what they could in their hometowns or in the nearest big city. Entire families moved into temporary houses (sometimes made of cardboard) that sprung up outside large cities. Because so many Americans blamed President Hoover for making the situation worse, these communities were called "Hoovervilles".

Living in these terrible conditions, people would cook what food they could get and would keep on going out every day to look for work. When gas got too expensive, they would use horses to pull their cars (called "Hoover Wagons"). When their shoes got holes in them, and they couldn't afford a new pair, they would stick a piece of cardboard inside and call it "Hoover leather". Can you see how difficult it was to live back then, and how so many Americans felt disappointed by the President's actions? Actually, President Hoover didn't think that it was the job of the federal government to get involved in the national economy. He felt that he should just step back and let the problem correct itself. Do you think that he was right? After all, it was the federal government who had made the situation much worse. They had passed the Smoot–Hawley Tariff Act a few years before and had slowed down American production!

When it came time to elect a new president in 1932, the nation overwhelmingly chose Franklin Delano Roosevelt, a man who had used his campaign to promise help for the struggling economy. One of the most important things for Roosevelt after being elected was to bring back the confidence of the American people. During his inaugural speech, he said the famous quote:

> "I am certain that my fellow Americans expect that on my induction into the Presidency I will address them with a candor and a decision which the present situation of our people impels. This is preeminently the time to speak the truth, the whole truth, frankly and boldly. Nor need we shrink from honestly facing conditions in our country today. This great Nation will endure as it has endured, will revive and will prosper. So, first of all, let me assert my firm belief that **the only thing we have to fear is fear itself**— nameless, unreasoning, unjustified terror which paralyzes needed efforts to convert retreat into advance."[1]

With this optimism in the future of the United States, President Roosevelt declared a four day bank holiday in order to help the strongest banks stay in business, and he started to have "fireside chats" (special radio broadcasts) that were aimed at talking directly with the American people and letting them know what he was doing to fix the bad economy. He would encourage Americans to write their political representatives and pass new laws to fix problems in the economy. During one of his fireside chats in May

[1] FDR speech excerpt: http://historymatters.gmu.edu/d/5057/

of 1933, he outlined what he called the "New Deal" program; something that he was sure would make a big difference. The New Deal was a series of laws that really helped to make the Great Depression go away (we will see some of those acts and laws in more detail in a little bit).

As each of these new laws passed, things got just a little bit better. However, in 1937, there was another national recession that scared a lot of people. It appears that the government itself actually played a role in this little recession, which erased the previous three years' worth of progress, by tightening the money supply and reducing government spending. The economy wouldn't fully recover until the Great Depression had ended a few years later.

The average American had lost most of his money during the Stock Market crash of 1929 and the Great Depression that followed. There was no work to be found, people were living on the streets, and the government didn't know exactly how to handle the situation. Country after country went through the same experience. It was a tough time to be alive.

Chapter 4: What was it like to be a kid during the Great Depression?

Can you imagine what it would have been like to have lived in a Hooverville during the Great Depression? You probably wouldn't have had a bed anymore- that would have been sold long ago in order to buy food. Most likely, you would sleep each night on the floor, maybe surrounded by little brothers and sisters, wearing the same clothes that you had worn all day long. Each day would be pretty much the same: you would wake up with your stomach growling, and wait for your dad to come home from the soup kitchen with a little bit of bread or some donuts for the family to share. After eating breakfast, you would put on your shoes (if you had any) and would go out to the street to look for work. That's right, even kids were expected to try to find work during the Great Depression. After all, families needed all the help that they could get.

For a long time, children had worked in factories together with their parents. In 1938, President Roosevelt signed a new law, called the Fair Labor Standards Act, which made it hard for kids to get work in a factory like they had done before. This was done for two reasons: to protect kids from the dangerous working conditions in factories and to open up more jobs for the adults who were looking for work. After the act had become a law, the only way for a kid to make some money was by working in the fields picking vegetables or even cotton.

It was not an easy life. Some kids back then even lost their parents to disease or accidents and had to live as orphans. A lot of them didn't like the new child labor laws. So they decided to run away and hop onto moving trains. They would live in boxcars and travel from one place to another, looking for people to help them out. These kids, called the "box car kids" would try to find something, anything, to make them happy again. It was a lonely life, and sometimes these kids felt that nobody loved them or understood them. Look at what some of the kids said about living on the rails; you can see the confused emotions in their words: "We thought it was the magic carpet... the click of the rails...romance"; "The end of the rainbow was always somewhere else and it kept us moving"; "Most of all I remember the loneliness. More than once I cried. I felt so sad, so utterly alone."[2]

Kids had to deal with the same problems as adults back then: it was a scary time. They had to worry about where their next meal would come from and who would give it to them. They had to worry about staying warm during the winters and staying safe during a time when there was lots of crime.

When President Roosevelt spoke on the radio during his fireside chats, do you think that you would have felt better? Well, President Roosevelt did a very good job of earning people's confidence, and lots of people did start to trust the banks after he became president in 1933. Production in factories went up after he was elected, and the rate of unemployment even went down a little bit. So, things did get better when he was in charge. But what do you think was the one thing that you would really want as a kid during the Great Depression? That's right: kids just wanted things to get back to normal. We all like having a sense of security, of knowing that we have a home and that there is food in the cupboard. The only way that would ever happen would be if the Great Depression finally came to an end.

Now, we should remember that the Great Depression lasted for 10 years. That means that some kids were born and raised during this time, always seeing their parents worried about money and looking for work.

[2] Box car kid quotes: http://www.erroluys.com/frontpage.htm

What do you think? Do you think that these kids, when they got older and had their own families, were often worried about money also? Do you think it changed the way that they looked at banks and at the Federal government? Absolutely.

In fact, a lot of young Americans who grew up during the Great Depression never fully trusted the government or the large banks ever again, even after things had returned to normal. Many of them preferred to hide their money at home or to just save and save and save, never spending any money on something if it wasn't absolutely necessary. Although they had survived the Great Depression, many kids who were alive during it never forgot it.

Chapter 5: How did the Great Depression end?

The Great Depression finally ended in 1940. That year, the rate of unemployment fell (meaning that more people had jobs again) and factories started to get busy getting people working and giving them paychecks. While there are of course many factors that were involved in ending the Great Depression, we will look at two of them: the New Deal pushed forward by President Roosevelt and the outbreak of World War II.

The New Deal. The New Deal was a series of laws and acts announced in May of 1933 and later passed by President Roosevelt and Congress in order to stimulate growth in the economy and to help end the Great Depression. They were focused on creating jobs, protecting Americans, and on helping the banks. For his first one hundred days in office, from March to June of 1933, FDR worked with congress to save the nation. As one political commentator of the time later said: "At the end of February we were a congeries of disorderly panic-stricken mobs and factions. In the hundred days from March to June we became again an organized nation confident of our power to provide for our own security and to control our own destiny."[3]

Let's look at a few of the laws passed during this period that helped to end the Great Depression.

The Federal Deposit Insurance Corporation (FDIC): This program was created in 1933 as part of the New Deal. It guaranteed the safety of deposits made with banks of up to $250,000. If anything should happen to the bank, the accountholder's money would be protected. This program helped to protect both banks and citizens from the devastating consequences of bank runs.

The Gold Reserve Act: Made into a law on January 30, 1934, this act was an important step in moving away from the gold standard. Do you remember how the gold standard made it difficult for the Federal

[3] Lippman quote source: http://en.wikipedia.org/wiki/New_Deal

Reserve to print more money and to help people pay off their debts? With this act and others, the government got more gold and then had more freedom to print money. This allowed them later to not base the value of their currency anymore on gold but rather on fixed rates established by the government. This let workers earn larger salaries to pay off their debts from the 1920s and the 1930s.

Social Security Act: This act protected people who had lost their jobs, who were older and could no longer work, and who were widows or orphans. With this new law, many of the people who had suffered so much during the Great Depression started to get real help from the government. They got money to help them buy food, they received help with housing, and even got jobs.

The National Labor Relations Act: Made into a law on July 5, 1935, this law allowed workers to form unions if they felt that they were being taken advantage of by their companies. Instead of having to work in dangerous conditions for small paychecks, the workers could now negotiate with their bosses for better pay and for better working conditions. This was a big step in getting industrial America productive and profitable again.

The Works Progress Administration: Beginning in 1935, this program helped upwards of three million Americans at a time to find well-paying jobs. They would take care of building facilities like schools, roads, and bridges in order to benefit the community and to make some money for their families. This program lasted until 1943, when most of the workers had gotten other jobs in wartime America.

These programs (and many others that were passed as part of Roosevelt's New Deal) helped the United States economy to get on its feet again. Instead of just living on the streets, looking for food, Americans were now working hard manufacturing quality products and constructing the nation's infrastructure (like roads, dams, bridges, and so on). Americans felt useful again, and for the first time in many years, they had enough money to buy the things that they needed. They had clothes, food, and a house of their own.

Although there was a brief recession in 1937, the upward climb out of the Great Depression was slow and steady. However, there was another big factor which brought American unemployment to an end: the outbreak of World War II.

The outbreak of World War II. In the late 1930s, American officials were starting to get worried about some of the more extreme politicians that they were seeing in Europe. Men like Adolf Hitler, chancellor of Germany, and Benito Mussolini, Prime Minister of Italy, had started to scare nearby nations with their aggressive words and threats. Hitler even spoke of a "Third Reich", or a third "kingdom", that Germany was destined to be head of. He felt that his people were a "master race" that should dominate the rest of the world.

President Roosevelt was afraid that a war was coming soon. In fact, after Hitler invaded Poland on September 1, 1939, thus starting World War II in Europe, the American government began making preparations of their own just in case they too had to fight. Although they did not join the war for almost two years, Americans got busy right away making tanks, planes, and guns in factories across the country. This created lots of new jobs. Although the U.S. government had to go into debt to pay all of those workers, it was money well spent, because it helped the economy to rebound. As all of the workers had more money, they started to spend it at local businesses, large and small. These businesses made greater profits, their stock prices went up, and everyone had what they needed.

Although the outbreak of World War II was not the single factor that ended the Great Depression, the jobs that it gave to unemployed Americans and the money they earned certainly were both very important to improving the economy. Yes, the Great Depression had finally ended, and America had survived!

Chapter 6: What happened after the Great Depression?

The Great Depression and its effects completely changed the world of the 20th century. For starters, do you remember one of the things that President Herbert Hoover wasn't too sure about when the Great Depression started? He wasn't too sure whether or not the Federal Government should get involved with the national economy. However, by the time that FDR was elected, the American people *demanded* that the government come to their rescue. FDR gave the people confidence and passed the series of acts called the New Deal, but this marked a turning point in American history: the Federal government would be a part of the everyday lives of its citizens.

Some of the framers of the U.S. Constitution (like Thomas Jefferson) had imagined a Federal Government that would be limited in how much it demanded of the people and how much of a role it played in their lives. However, after the Great Depression, there were laws that governed how people worked, how they invested their money, and even how they lived after they retired or when they we having a rough time economically. These laws weren't necessarily a bad thing, but they did change forever the role of the government in people's lives.

Also, many groups that had been divided socially and politically before the Great Depression found themselves working together for the same goals during it. For example, African Americans, whites, rich and poor, all suffered together during the 1930s, and they had to learn to work together in order to solve the problems. After the Great Depression, many social problems had been solved.

Most of the Federal programs that were created by the New Deal are still around today. For example, Social Security still helps retired Americans, and the FDIC still protects our investments in banks today. We can be glad that these programs are around, because they are helping the United States economy so that another Great Depression never comes.

There were also some very sad consequences of the Great Depression, however. We already talked about how difficult it was to be alive back then. The American people were desperate to find a leader who would help them to solve their problems. They wanted someone who would take charge and guide their nation into more prosperous times. President Roosevelt did this by having fireside chats with his fellow Americans and by passing helpful legislation thorough to make it into law. However, things were quite different in Germany.

Germany, after World War I, had a lot of "reparations" (penalties) to pay to the nations that it had attacked. This made things very tough in their economy. When the Smoot–Hawley Tariff Act was passed in 1930 and then the Great Depression came, the national economy completely collapsed. Their currency became worthless, and people would burn money because it was cheaper than burning wood. Like Americans of the same time, the German people were looking for someone who would inspire them with confidence and who would lead them back into more prosperous time. They thought that they had found such a man in Adolf Hitler.

The Great Depression had created the perfect environment for a leader like Adolf Hitler. He used people's fears and uncertainties about the future to his advantage, to promote his own personal beliefs. Unfortunately, many people died as a result of World War II, which was started mainly by Adolf Hitler and his twisted ideas. This was the saddest consequence of all from the Great Depression.

Finally, as we mentioned before, an entire generation had been raised during the Great Depression. After having lived for so long without work, when they finally got a job after the depression had ended, they were likely to stay with the employer for their whole lives, grateful to have a steady paycheck. Also, they (unlike their parents from the roaring twenties) would probably spend the rest of their lives being very thrifty and teaching their children the value of a dollar.

Conclusion

The Great Depression was a very difficult time not only for Americans, but also for people living in the whole world. Do you remember how it started?

The Great Depression began as a normal recession in the summer of 1929. However, as investors saw that stock prices weren't going down, but instead were being driven higher and higher by speculation, they started to lose their confidence in the national economy. On Tuesday, October 29, 1929 (called "Black Tuesday") the Stock Market crashed. As a result, companies closed their doors, Americans were stuck with no jobs and large debts, and banks were run on and eventually were forced to close their doors too. American workers lost their cars, their homes, and sometimes even their families. They had to wait in long lines to get a small bowl of soup, and some even had to move into little cardboard communities called "Hoovervilles".

Things started to get better when President Roosevelt came into office in 1933. Right away, he made sure that helpful laws, protecting banks, companies, and American citizens, were passed. He made sure there wouldn't be any more bank runs, and he finally did away with the gold standard. These changes helped the economy to improve steadily until World War II broke out in 1939, when American wartime preparations took over and helped to provide much-needed jobs and paychecks to Americans everywhere.

Although America had survived the Great Depression, there were a lot of hard lessons learned along the way. For example, one of them had to do with the way that we invest in the Stock Market. It was learned that wild speculation is never a good idea, especially with borrowed money. A saying was born that is true to this day: "If you can't afford to lose it, don't invest it." Investors who follow this advice will never go into debt because of a recession or a stock market crash.

Another lesson had to do with the best way to get out of a recession/depression. Do you remember what both Presidents Hoover and Roosevelt tried to do? They did the same as most American citizens: save money and try to limit spending. However, that's kind of like holding medicine in your hand when you're sick instead of swallowing it and expecting to feel better. Without medicine, we can't get better; without money, the economy won't improve. Really, the government should have been spending money and cutting taxes instead of raising taxes and saving money. The Great Depression could have been much less severe and much shorter if this had been done.

During the recession that began in 2008, President Barack Obama tried to show that he had learned some lessons from the Great Depression. In order to prevent the recession from getting worse, Federal interest rates on loans were lowered in order to make it easier for individuals and companies to get the money they needed for their businesses and purchases. Banks were "bailed out" (helped) to make sure that they didn't collapse, and tax cuts from the previous presidency were extended. Because of these and other smart decisions, the recession was not as severe as it could have been, and a global depression was avoided.

The Great Depression lasted for nearly ten years, but the lessons that we have learned from it will last forever. We have learned how quickly things can change in our lives and not to take anything for granted. What about you? What lessons have you learned from the Great Depression?

Made in the USA
Coppell, TX
31 October 2019